This book belongs to:

It is in giving that we receive.

–*St. Francis of Assisi*

Gooseberry Patch
2500 Farmers Dr., #110
Columbus, OH 43235

www.gooseberrypatch.com
1·800·854·6673

Copyright 2011, Gooseberry Patch 978-1-936283-93-4
First Printing, May, 2011

Tiny Tips
for
Gifts to Make & Give

Caramel Nut
Cake

Dedication

*To all of our friends,
who make it such a pleasure to
give from the heart.*

Enjoy!

*A gift from the kitchen
is a gift from the heart.*

– Unknown

For an extra-special gift, wrap up a jar
of homemade jam in a lacy vintage handkerchief
and tie it with a ribbon.

Tie sprigs of rosemary, for remembrance,
to jars of jams & jellies before giving.

A thoughtful gift...a soothing chamomile tea bath!
Fill a cheesecloth bag with chamomile flowers
and tie. Hanging from a bathtub faucet, running
water will release its sweet fragrance.

Make a bath mitten! Fold a washcloth
in half; sew two of the sides closed,
leaving one side open. Sew on a loop
and place a bar of soap inside.

Ribbon-covered buttons are so pretty when used to decorate packages, and covered-button kits can be found at any craft or fabric store.

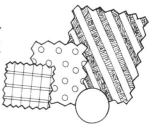

Simply wrap each button top with ribbon, then snap on the back. It's so easy!

Too sweet...wrap packages in plain red
wrapping paper and glue a row or two
of wrapped red & white peppermints
all across the top.

Give a garden in a can!
Fill a vintage watering can with
a variety of flower, vegetable and
herb seeds...add some gloves, a few garden
markers and a gardening magazine.

Here's another way to inspire a friend to
think spring! Paint a terra-cotta pot
to match a pretty pair of gloves and
tuck in seed packets and a new trowel.

A retro breadbox is a great way to share a warm loaf of homemade bread. Add a crock of butter too!

Surprise a teacher with an apple-filled vintage lunch box! Tuck in apple-shaped sugar cookies, apple muffins and a jar of homemade apple butter.

A gift for the person who has
everything...a retro tin lunchbox featuring
his or her favorite childhood cartoon character!
Fill it with homemade cookies and old-fashioned
candies...he or she will feel just like a kid again.

Do you know someone who loves to bake?
Fill a fabric-lined basket or mixing bowl with
all the ingredients for a favorite cake mix recipe.
Tuck in a spatula and tie on a recipe card
for an oh-so-welcome gift!

**The only gift is a portion
of thyself.**

–*Ralph Waldo Emerson*

Give a roll of sugar cookies with the decorations included. Yummy chocolate-dipped raisins, bright sparkly sugars and sprinkles make cookie-baking fun!

Slice 'n Bake
Sugar Cookie Dough

Pair a cookie mix with a baking sheet, jars of colored sugar, sprinkles and jimmies...a gift that's just right for a sweet friend.

Chocolate Covered Raisin Cookie Mix

A friend who bakes would love to find a cookbook slipped in the pocket of a potholder. Don't forget to tuck in recipe cards sharing some family favorites too.

Vintage napkins can often be found at
tag sales...use them as special wrapping paper
for gifts from your kitchen!

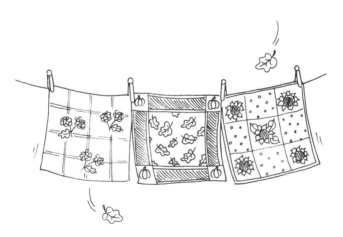

Color copies of vintage fabrics make
terrific one-of-a-kind stationery,
scrapbook pages, envelopes or gift tags.

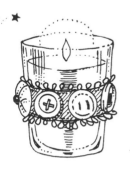

Use craft glue to adhere colorful buttons around a plain glass votive holder...a quick-as-a-wink gift anyone is sure to love.

Fill a large pickle jar with a pillar candle, then surround it with an assortment of colorful buttons. A whimsical present for a crafty friend!

Fill delicate flowered vintage teacups
with scented wax crystals and slip in a wick.
These sweet candles are nice to have on hand
for special visitors!

Give a jar of your homemade
preserves with a loaf of warm bread
wrapped in a pretty linen towel.

Wrap a wide gingham ribbon around a freshly baked loaf of Italian bread and a wooden breadboard...a heartwarming gift for a good friend.

Whip up a new tablecloth or runner and matching napkins from homespun...no sewing needed! To add a fringe, just pull away threads, one row at a time. A cheery gift!

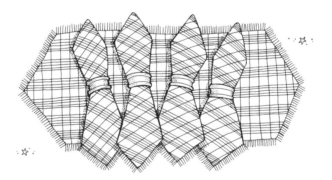

Homemade from the heart! Photocopy favorite snapshots onto iron-on transfer paper available at craft and office supply stores. Iron onto crisp white fabric, frame with a ribbon border and sew into a pillow. It's "sew" easy!

Handmade tags are perfect for homemade jar mixes.
Use cookie cutters as patterns...just trace around your
favorite, cut out and add the finishing touches!
Dress up your tags with vintage buttons or yo-yos.

Fill vintage-style milk bottles with homemade
cocoa, set them in a wire milk bottle carrier
and deliver to friends...what a tasty gift!

A vintage thermos is a clever way to give
cocoa, coffee or cider mix too.

A college student's dream!
Fill airtight containers with
cookies, brownies and bars.
Send during exam week for
a tasty study break. Look
for containers in school
colors or decorate the package
with spirited stickers!

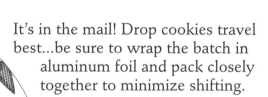

It's in the mail! Drop cookies travel
best...be sure to wrap the batch in
aluminum foil and pack closely
together to minimize shifting.

Package a gift of cookies in a jiffy!
Decorate a cardboard mailing tube with
stickers or cut-outs and slide in a
plastic-wrapped stack of cookies.

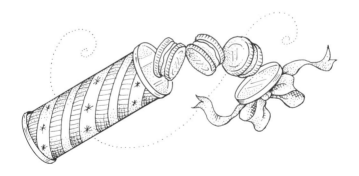

Découpage color copies of
photos onto a package for
one-of-a-kind giftwrap!

*Give the world the best that you have,
and the best will come back to you.*

–Madeline Bridges

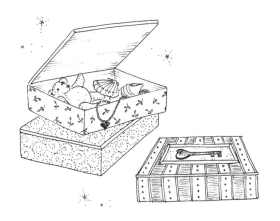

Decorate a pocket-size candy tin
as a delightful container for a gift of
jewelry. Add color with craft spray paint and
découpage a vintage cut-out on the lid.
It's sure to be treasured.

A friend who loves scrapbooking will be thrilled to receive a gift bag filled with decorative-edged scissors, tags, stickers, buttons, ribbons and rubber stamps.

Surprise a crafty friend with a jazzy journal. Dress up the cover of a blank journal with scrapbooking paper, buttons, charms and bits of ribbon... how charming!

Homebaked goodies are always welcome. For a fun and frugal presentation, run brightly colored leftover wrapping paper through a paper shredder. Use it to fill a gift box and tuck in a stack of plastic-wrapped cookies.

Keep a look-out for cake molds at yard sales and flea markets. They're great for filling with cupcakes and cookies...wrap with cellophane and top with a bow.

Edge a colorful paper plate with pinking shears and top with sheets of tissue paper. Arrange cookies on top and then slide the plate into a cellophane bag. Tied up with a big ribbon, it makes a simply yummy gift!

Have friends,
not for the sake
of receiving,
but of giving.

– Joseph Roux

Spell out names on gift tags with simple letter stamps or stickers to give presents an old-fashioned feeling. Make tags extra special with rick-rack, buttons and ribbon!

Whip up a snuggly fleece blanket in no time at all. Cut fleece to any size and use scissors to add a fringe to the edge...so easy, and no sewing needed!

Add a sweet touch to plain cloth napkins.
Use a simple straight embroidery stitch to
add a guest's initial to each napkin, then
finish off the edges with a blanket stitch.

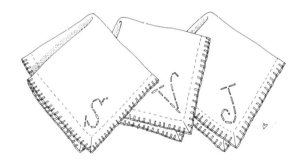

Toss in a few fresh tomatoes from the garden when giving away a jar of salsa, and don't forget to include the recipe!

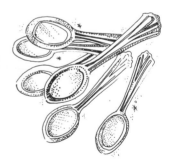

Keep an eye out for vintage silver spoons at flea markets...oh-so clever tied onto giftable jars of salsa, jam, jelly or relish.

Homemade jams & jellies are always welcome and make yummy gifts! Wrap the jars with raffia then glue an old-fashioned yo-yo on the bow. Top the yo-yo with a vintage button.

Big and roomy, vintage bags and hat boxes
are terrific tag-sale finds. Use one for tucking
in lots of little surprises...a girlfriend
will be delighted!

A gift any new mom will really love!
Search flea markets or book shops for
old-fashioned nursery rhyme books in
less-than-perfect condition. They're filled with
charming pictures that
would be darling framed in
a baby's room!

Vintage shops turn up the prettiest treasures.
A glittery brooch or an old-fashioned button
pinned to the center of a bow will
really make a special package sparkle.

*The manner of giving is
worth more than the gift.*

–Pierre Corneille

Homemade coupons make great gifts for the whole family. How about a coupon volunteering to be a young teen's personal taxi service on a Friday night?

A button bookmark makes a sweet gift for any book lover on your gift list. Stitch buttons of different sizes onto a satin ribbon, then unravel and knot the ends to create a fringe.

Make a keepsake box for a close friend or sister.
Cover the lid of a round shaker box with vintage
buttons, yo-yo's or charms. An old spool in the
middle would make a perfect knob for the box.
Add a small frame with a favorite photograph
of the two of you.

A welcome housewarming gift for new neighbors!
Prepare a quick & easy family favorite in a new casserole
dish...enclose the recipe along with a note that says
the dish is theirs to keep. Add a few more recipes
tucked inside a giftable oven mitt.

Tasty casseroles are welcome gifts for new parents.
Make several and deliver them before the baby
arrives. They can freeze them now, then simply
pop dinner in the oven to bake later.

**A joy that's shared
is a joy made double.**

–English Proverb

When preparing layered mixes be sure to pack each layer down firmly. Use a large spoon or even a small drinking glass to press layers down. This way, all the layers will fit perfectly in the jar!

Give everything a second glance...it may be just right for gift giving. Mixes can be tucked inside berry baskets, jelly jars, flower pots and even coffee cans!

Wrapped in love! Use children's drawings as wrapping paper for family birthdays, anniversaries and other celebrations. Perfect for grandparents and aunts & uncles.

Table linens or tea towels are terrific for wrapping gifts...and the wrapping becomes a lasting present too.

Look for whimsical giftwrap in unexpected places! Road maps and brown kraft paper are wonderful for wrapping big presents, while scrapbooking and origami paper are just the right size for smaller packages.

Personalized votives are a snap to make. Cut a piece of parchment paper to fit around a votive holder. Write names on the parchment paper with a felt-tip pen. Simply wrap paper around votive and secure with double-sided tape.

It's simple to give votive holders a frosty look.
Coat holders with spray adhesive, then roll in
mica snow. Candles tucked inside will glimmer.

A big popcorn tin is easily turned into a just-right gift for the movie lover on your list! Spray the tin with craft paint and découpage with movie star photos from magazines. Tuck in a DVD, a movie magazine and some snacks for a fun evening in. Turn over the tin's lid and it becomes a handy serving tray!

A lollipop bouquet! Fit florists' foam into a new terra-cotta pot and slip cookie pops securely into the foam. Cover the foam with colorful crinkled paper...what a kid-pleasing treat!

Pressed flowers are easy to make at home...just sandwich blooms between tissue paper and cardboard. Set a heavy book and a brick on top and wait about two weeks. Perfect for crafts and decorating!

Fill an oversized mug with pens, pencils, sticky notes and some tea bags. What a clever way to say "congrats" to a friend on landing a new job!

Mix up this soothing tea blend and delight a busy
friend. Combine one cup each of organic chamomile
and lavender flowers from a health food store. Place in
a decorative jar and tie on a tea infuser spoon with
a ribbon. Add some homemade cookies to
enjoy too...so thoughtful!

Make your gift wrapping truly special without spending a penny! Ask your local wallpaper store for discontinued sample books, usually given away. Use the colorful, fun variety of wallpapers to wrap small gifts, or to decorate the larger packages with plaids, stripes, flowers and scenery.

**In the sweetness of friendship
let there be laughter,
and sharing of pleasures.**

–Kahlil Gibran

A bucket or vintage lunch pail overflowing with a favorite snack will be a welcome gift! Fill it with a variety of nuts, sweet treats or packages of microwave popcorn.

Heading to dinner at a friend's house? Line a pail with a kitchen towel, tuck in some freshly baked breadsticks and a bottle of dipping oil. A tasty treat and so thoughtful.

When you give goodies in clever containers, they
become part of the gift! Antique fluted pudding molds,
old-fashioned tea cups and tea pots, hatboxes or
vintage cookie jars are just right for gift-giving.
Add your treat inside then wrap with holiday
ribbon or lengths of dimestore rickrack.

Create a personal herb garden! Choose a narrow wooden crate that will fit on a windowsill. Fill it with starter pots of herbs...rosemary, basil, oregano and thyme make a yummy kitchen sampler.

Top off a giftable garden book with a bouquet of beautiful hydrangeas you dried last summer...a sweet gift from the heart.

Passing along a thimbleful of flower seeds to a friend makes a cheery gift. Place them inside plain envelopes, and then bundle several envelopes together with vintage ribbon.

Fill whimsical retro salt & pepper shakers with salt blends and rubs...don't forget to attach a favorite recipe for a tasty gift any cook will appreciate.

Gather a variety of barbecue sauces, marinades and rubs in a painted pail. Take along for the hostess of a backyard gathering...guests will love trying them out!

A jar of honey is a sweet addition to the
breakfast table to enjoy on hot biscuits, toast or
pancakes...even drizzled in a steamy cup of hot tea.
Pick up flavors like orange blossom and wildflower
at a farmers' market. Be sure to add a
wooden honey dipper too!

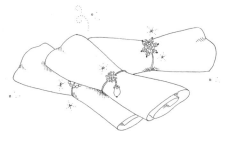

Bits of vintage jewelry and faux flowers really dress up a plain napkin. Slide pint-size trinkets over metallic silver or gold thread, then tie on. How charming!

Old-fashioned swanky swig glasses make the prettiest tealight holders. Candlelight inside lets their colorful, retro designs really shine through!

A very special gift for a young lady! Line an
old-fashioned hatbox with an eyelet-edged tea towel
and add cookies, a packet of spiced teabags and
a dainty teacup & saucer set.

Create a gift bag with a window. Cut a shape from the front of the bag and glue cellophane or plastic wrap on the inside to cover the opening...a sneak peek at the treats!

Don't throw out those plain paper bags! Just add a colorful piece of tissue paper, a vintage postcard and a ribbon bow for a brand-new look.

Hold a true friend
with both hands.

–*Kanuri Proverb*

Just for fun, turn vintage jelly glasses into candles. Holding a wick in place, pour scented wax gel into each glass. They're especially pretty with gels in glowing "jelly" colors like red and amber!

Handmade soaps found at country fairs and craft shows make such thoughtful gifts. Keep the packaging simple but special by placing one or two blocks of soap on an ironstone dish, add a washcloth and tie up with ribbon.

It's easy to turn a vintage painted metal tray
into a whimsical wall clock with a clock kit from
your local craft store. Drill a center hole, then insert
the clock movement and hands. Press on
self-adhesive numbers...time's up!

Make a gift of homemade candy even sweeter...place
individual candies in mini paper muffin cups
and arrange in a decorated box.

"Stay" is a charming word
in a friend's vocabulary.

–Louisa May Alcott

Buy an inexpensive plastic truck or wagon at a toy store...fill the bed with candy and tie on a tag that says, "To a friend who's loads of fun!"

Sweet wrapping in a snap! Decorate a paper sack with stencils or rubber stamps and fill with candy. Fold the top over, punch two holes and slide a peppermint stick through.

Decorate a frosty glass jar to fill with goodies.
Choose a clear glass jar and press on round stickers.
Following package directions, apply etching cream to jar,
covering completely. Peel off stickers when finished
to reveal your one-of-a-kind design!

Make leaf rubbings for fun and easy wrapping paper and placemats! Arrange leaves face-down on plain white paper and cover with another sheet of paper. Remove wrappers from crayons and rub over the leaves...their images will magically appear.

If you know someone who's a music lover, use sheet music for wrapping gift boxes. Look for single pages of nostalgic tunes at flea markets or tag sales.

Lighten up a little...cover packages in the Sunday comics or a page of crossword puzzles, just for fun!

Just a dab of hot glue, some ribbon and vintage baubles can transform ordinary silverware into something extraordinary.

Make a sparkling beaded bracelet for a little girl...so easy! Beads can be found at craft shops, and ribbons to string them on come in endless colors. Clasps are attached to the ribbon at each end with a simple knot. To give, wrap around a pretty vintage hankie for a surprise she's sure to remember.

Turn a wooden birdhouse from the craft store
into a sweet tissue holder! Carefully pull the
roof loose and reattach it on one side with
two small hinges. Paint the birdhouse, then
slip a tissue box inside and pull tissues
through the hole in front.

Vellum bags turn simple treats into extra-special gifts...look for them at a craft or stationery store.

Kindness is
never wasted.

–S. H. Simmons

Celebrate Good Neighbor Day by
hand-delivering a cheery potted fall mum
to a neighbor. It's always on September 28.

Giving a gift card for a birthday or other
special occasion? Make it memorable when you
slip the card into a festive take-out container alongside
some cello-wrapped homemade cookies. Tie curling
ribbons to the handle. How sweet!

Fill an oversized mug with some flavored tea bags and a new tea ball...give along with a good book for an afternoon of relaxation.

Perfect for a true-blue friend...fill a basket with blue washcloths, a big blue fluffy towel, some fuzzy blue slippers and a big bag of chocolate chip cookies.

Children's sand pails can often be found at antique shops. Filled with a bag of a snack mix and a new sand shovel for scooping, it's an ideal hostess gift for a summertime get-together.

Decorate a cookie plate...what a clever idea!
Stamp the back of a clear glass plate, using white or
silver acrylic paint and a star-shaped foam craft stamp.
Allow to dry, then set paint as indicated on label.

Charming! Turn a gift box into a
keepsake by using satin ribbons to
cover the sides and bottom. Use a
basket-weave pattern with several
ribbons to cover the lid.

A new twist for packages...add a homemade pompom in place of a paper bow. Simply wind yarn tightly around a 4-inch cardboard square several times. Holding carefully, slide yarn off cardboard and tie in the center with an 8-inch length of yarn. Clip the looped ends and shake out to fluff.

Dresser drawer sachets make quick & easy gifts! Sew tiny pillows of homespun fabric or wide ribbon, place a bit of fragrant potpourri inside and stitch closed.

A simple-to-make gift...little sleep pillows. Stitch together two flowered hankies on three sides and fill with dried herbs like chamomile, dill, lavender and peppermint. Stitch closed and tuck into your pillowcase for sweet dreams.

Make crafty cut-out coasters for friends & family...it's
simple using 5-inch squares of wool felt. Use a hole punch
to make designs in one square of felt, then top it with
fusible webbing cut the same size. Place a second square
of felt over the webbing and iron to fuse the pieces together.
Trim the edges with pinking or scallop shears.

A homemade checkerboard that will make everyone feel like a winner...découpage a grandchild's picture over every other square of a prepainted checkerboard. Copy and reduce pictures, if necessary, using a color photocopier.

Pets are a part of the family, too! Your friends will be touched if you remember their pet with a small gift of dog biscuits or a catnip toy.

The road to a friend's house
is never long.

–Danish Proverb

Our Story

Back in 1984, we were next-door neighbors raising our families in the little town of Delaware, Ohio. Two moms with small children, we were looking for a way to do what we loved and stay home with the kids too. We had always shared a love of home cooking and making memories with family & friends and so, after many a conversation over the backyard fence, **Gooseberry Patch** was born.

We put together our first catalog at our kitchen tables, enlisting the help of our loved ones wherever we could. From that very first mailing, we found an immediate connection with many of our customers and it wasn't long before we began receiving letters, photos and recipes from these new friends. In 1992, we put together our very first cookbook, compiled from hundreds of these recipes and, the rest, as they say, is history.

Hard to believe it's been over 25 years since those kitchen-table days! From that original little **Gooseberry Patch** family, we've grown to include an amazing group of creative folks who love cooking, decorating and creating as much as we do.
Today, we're best known for our homestyle, family-friendly cookbooks, now recognized as national bestsellers.

One thing's for sure, we couldn't have done it without our friends all across the country. Each year, we're honored to turn thousands of your recipes into our collectible cookbooks. Our hope is that each book captures the stories and heart of all of you who have shared with us. Whether you've been with us since the beginning or are just discovering us, welcome to the **Gooseberry Patch** family!

JoAnn & Vickie

Visit our website anytime
www.gooseberrypatch.com
1·800·854·6673

Since 1992, we've been publishing our bestselling cookbooks for every kitchen and every meal of the day! With hundreds of budget-friendly recipes using ingredients you already have on hand, their lay-flat binding makes them easy to use. Each is filled with hand-drawn artwork and plenty of personality.

Have a taste for more?

We created our official Circle of Friends so we could fill everyone in on the latest scoop at once. Visit us online to join in the fun and discover free recipes, exclusive giveaways and much more!

www.gooseberrypatch.com

Join Our Circle of Friends

Find Gooseberry Patch in Your Neighborhood

f Find us on Facebook

You Tube

Follow us on **twitter**

Read Our Blog